SESAME STREET®

TOUGH TOPICS

Talking about
Incarceration

A Sesame Street
Resource

Marie-Therese Miller

Lerner Publications ◆ Minneapolis

Dear Grown-Up,

The more comfortable you are talking with children about the challenges they face, the more of a difference you can make in their lives. In this series, *Sesame Street* friends provide caregivers and educators a starting point to discuss, process, and offer support on tough topics. Together, we can help kids learn coping and resilience-building techniques to help them face tough challenges such as divorce, grief, and more.

Sincerely,
the Editors at Sesame Workshop

Table of Contents

What Is Incarceration?

Being incarcerated means a person is in jail or prison. They can't be with you. People go to prison because they may have broken a grown-up rule called a law.

Hi, I'm Alex. My dad is in prison and I miss him a lot.

In courtrooms, judges decide if a person will go to prison or jail and for how long.

If someone you love is in prison, it's not your fault.

When I'm sad, Granny Bird gives me good hugs.

When someone you love is incarcerated, you might feel sad, scared, or angry. It's okay to have all of these big feelings.

You have people who love and care for you.

You can talk to them.

When I don't understand something, I ask Papi.

Staying in Touch

You can keep in touch with the person you love while they are in prison. You might color a picture or have someone help you write a letter.

A grown-up can help you mail the letter to your loved one.

My dad and I write letters to each other.

Sometimes the person you love can write you letters too. They might call you on the phone or video chat with you.

You might be able to visit the person you love. You may need to wait in a line. You might see people wearing uniforms too.

A grown-up can tell you what to expect before you visit.

During the visit, you might talk about school or something fun you did. You can share things you're learning or sing them a song!

When I visit my dad, I tell him all about my favorite things in school.

Even though the person you love can't be with you, you can keep them in your heart.

Your person knows that you love them!

What You Can Do

You can draw a picture of yourself doing something fun and send it to your person in prison. You might create a drawing of you at the playground or at school with friends.

Glossary

courtrooms: places where people talk about laws, which are grown-up rules, and what should happen if people have broken them

judges: people who help make a decision about whether a person should go to prison

prison: a building that people live in when they may have broken a law

uniforms: special clothes to show that a group of people live or work together

Read More

Felice, Frank. *What Happens When My Parent Is in Jail?* New York: PowerKids, 2019.

Greenwood, Sara. *My Brother Is Away.* New York: Random House Studio, 2022.

Miller, Marie-Therese. *How Are You Feeling? Naming Your Emotions with Sesame Street.* Minneapolis: Lerner Publications, 2023.

Explore more resources that help kids (and grown-ups!) provided by Sesame Workshop, the nonprofit educational organization behind Sesame Street. Visit https://sesameworkshop.org/tough-topics/.

Photo Acknowledgments

Image credits: Michael Macor/The San Francisco Chronicle via Getty Images, p. 4; gorodenkoff/Getty Images, p. 6; ilkercelik/Getty Images, p. 9; shapecharge/Getty Images, p. 10; The Good Brigade/Getty Images, p. 11; Chatchai Limjareon/Getty Images, p. 12; ArtMarie/Getty Images, p. 13; Mehmet Hilmi Barcin/Getty Images, p. 14; Peter Berglund/Getty Images, p. 16; Michael Macor/The San Francisco Chronicle via Getty Images, p. 18 (top); Spencer Weiner/Los Angeles Times via Getty Images, p. 18 (center); AP Photo/Rich Pedroncelli, p. 18 (bottom); In Pictures Ltd./Corbis via Getty Images, p. 19; Pollyana Ventura/Getty Images, p. 21.

Cover: Douglas Sacha/Getty Images.

Index

To the children who love someone in prison

Lerner Publications Company
An imprint of Lerner Publishing Group, Inc.
241 First Avenue North
Minneapolis, MN 55401 USA

For reading levels and more information, look up this title at www.lernerbooks.com.

Main body text set in Mikado. Typeface provided by HVD.

Library of Congress Cataloging-in-Publication Data

Names: Miller, Marie-Therese, author.
Title: Talking about incarceration : a Sesame Street resource / Marie-Therese Miller.
Description: Minneapolis : Lerner Publications, [2024] | Series: Sesame Street tough topics | Includes bibliographical references and index. | Audience: Ages 4–8 | Audience: Grades K–1 | Summary: "Friends from Sesame Street help young readers understand what to expect when a loved one is incarcerated. Readers learn how to stay in touch with their loved one, that their feelings are valid, and more"— Provided by publisher.
Identifiers: LCCN 2023035599 (print) | LCCN 2023035600 (ebook) | ISBN 9798765620175 (library binding) | ISBN 9798765629703 (paperback) | ISBN 9798765637487 (epub)
Subjects: LCSH: Imprisonment—Juvenile literature. | Prisons—Juvenile literature.
Classification: LCC HV8705 .M55 2024 (print) | LCC HV8705 (ebook) | DDC 365—dc23/eng/20231107

LC record available at https://lccn.loc.gov/2023035599
LC ebook record available at https://lccn.loc.gov/2023035600

Manufactured in the United States of America
1-1009961-51822-11/27/2023